THE AUTHORSHIP OF HEBREWS

THE CASE FOR PAUL

DAVID ALAN BLACK

Energion Publications
Gonzalez, FL
2013

Unless otherwise noted, scripture translations are by the author.

ISBN10: 1-938434-73-0
ISBN13: 978-1-938434-73-0

Energion Publications
P. O. Box 841
Gonzalez, FL 32560

energionpubs.com
pubs@energion.com

PREFACE

This book is a popularization of several essays of mine published in academic journals. Here I have tried to avoid over-technical language that academic scholars might deem essential, and I have transliterated all Greek terms to meet the needs of ordinary educated people. I am grateful to Mr. Henry Neufeld of Energion Publications for accepting this work into his series *Topical Line Drives*. I am also grateful to my personal assistant, Mr. Jacob Cerone, for his editorial assistance.

Many scholars have insisted that Paul could not have authored Hebrews. I hope my brief treatise will show that they are quite possibly wrong. At the very least, my prayer is that this book will help jumpstart the conversation. I dedicate it with love to all my Hebrews students, past, present, and future.

INTRODUCTION

The question "Who wrote the epistle of Paul to the Hebrews?" is, as Ray Stedman and others have quipped, akin to asking "Who is buried in Grant's tomb?" The traditional author, as reflected in the letter's superscription in the *Authorized Version*,[1] is of course the apostle Paul, but hardly any scholar of late would agree with this traditional assessment. Indeed, that Hebrews is non-Pauline is now considered one of the "assured results" of scholarly research.[2] During my seminary days and well into my graduate studies I adhered to this consensus view. However, Pauline authorship was defended by William Leonard in *The Authorship of the Epistle to the Hebrews* published in 1939,[3] since which time it cannot so

1 In the AV the epistle has the heading, "Epistle of Paul the Apostle to the Hebrews." In early mss. of the NT the heading reads simply, "To the Hebrews."
2 R. C. H. Lenski flatly states: "Paul did not write Hebrews" (*The Interpretation of the Epistle to the Hebrews and the Epistle of James* [Minneapolis: Augsburg, 1966] 8). More recently, H. W. Attridge has asserted: "As is generally recognized today, whoever wrote Hebrews, it was certainly not Paul" (*The Epistle to the Hebrews* [Hermeneia; Philadelphia: Fortress, 1989] 2).
3 William Leonard, *The Authorship of the Epistle to the Hebrews: Critical Problem and Use of the Old Testament* (Rome: Vatican Polyglot Press, 1939). Pauline authorship was also defended by M. Stuart, *A Commentary on the Epistle to the Hebrews* (2d. ed.; Andover: Flagg, Gould, and Newman, 1833); R. Milligan, *The New Testament Commentary: Epistle to the Hebrews* (St. Louis: Christian

easily be brushed aside. Indeed, a recent study by Andrew W. Pitts and Joshua F. Walker has challenged the *consensus opinio* by reexamining the raw data, drawing heavily from my previously published work on the subject. Their essay is entitled "The Authorship of Hebrews: A Further Development in the Luke-Paul Relationship."[4] In it they conclude that Hebrews is "Pauline" in a very real sense, in that Luke took a discourse given by Paul in a diaspora synagogue and subsequently published it as a written text. They write, "Although Hebrews has been handed down to us without an author, we have argued that both external and internal considerations suggest that Hebrews constitutes Pauline speech material, recorded and later published by Luke, Paul's traveling companion."[5] In my view, this essay marks a milestone in contemporary Hebrews research. Few have attempted this kind of close scrutiny of the text because it necessitates a highly critical stance toward recent tradition, in this case at least a century of tradition that has rejected the Paulinity of Hebrews. I am grateful for essays like this one. They ask us to "revision" the text in ways that are perhaps more faithful to the evidence, both external and internal. Revisioning is a difficult process. It is difficult because it is hard for us to look past our own traditional blinders in the light of serious exegesis. It can create dissonance between ourselves and our theological heritage. It is fraught with problems and challenges. Yet the rewards can be remarkably satisfying.[6]

In Part 1 of this work we will reexamine the internal evidence for Pauline authorship, concentrating on the letter's language and style, while in a Part 2 we will analyze the statements of the earliest Christian fathers concerning the authorship of Hebrews. Our contention is that there is strong (though not probative) internal evidence and solid external evidence for the Paulinity of the epistle.

Publishing Co., 1875); cf. J. Phillips, *Exploring the Scriptures* (Chicago: Moody, 1965) 268-69.

4 *Paul and His Social Relations*, eds. Stanley E. Porter and Christopher D. Land (Leiden: Brill, 2013) 143-84.

5 Ibid., 183-84.

6 In the words of William Leonard, who himself doubted direct Pauline authorship before examining the data, "Many indications are forthcoming that true progress very often means a return to positions which we should have never left" (*Authorship*, 387).

PART 1: THE INTERNAL EVIDENCE

The question we wish to pose in Part 1 is this: In view of the letter's unique language and elegance of style, does a scrutiny of the contacts between Hebrews and the Pauline letters confirm the view, clearly voiced at Alexandria by Pantaenus and the ἀρχαῖοι ἄνδρες (*archaioi andres*) whose lives went back before the middle of the second century, that the epistle had Paul for its author? The use of internal evidence to prove the authorship of a NT book has always been a complex matter. In investigating the authorship of this epistle we must bear in mind that we are dealing with a balance of probabilities, which means that our conclusions must of necessity be comprised at times of indirect and incidental evidences. It is generally asserted that Hebrews has little, if anything, in common with the Pauline writings. Although stylistic features are often taken into account, conceptual factors are generally considered decisive. Certain dissimilarities between Hebrews and the writings of Paul are invoked in opposition to Pauline authorship. These include the absence both of the author's name and a salutation in the letter opening (1:1-4), the reference to the author's position as a secondhand recipient of tradition (2:3), the treatment of Jesus as high priest, and the sacerdotal imagery of Hebrews.

OVERLOOKED AFFINITIES BETWEEN HEBREWS AND PAUL

The dissimilarities mentioned above are widely acknowledged and have been discussed at length in the literature. What is less often stressed is the significant number of similarities between Hebrews and Paul. There is in fact a great deal of evidence that creates a strong presumption of affinity between Hebrews and the Pauline corpus. These similarities—conceptual and otherwise—certainly do exist, and a brief listing of them here may serve a useful purpose for anyone interested in investigating the matter of authorship.

» Attribution to Paul is reflected in canonical lists and manuscripts, including P[46] (c. 200), where it appears after Romans.[7] Why would a large segment of the early church add Hebrews to the Pauline corpus,

---

7 In the NT manuscript tradition Hebrews was *always* transmitted in association with the Pauline letters, although it occupies three different positions in that tradition. In our oldest uncials (א A B C) it follows 2 Thessalonians and

3

and not only to that, but put it next to the apostle's chief epistle, if Hebrews was not already considered a *Pauline* writing? Precisely because the letter lacks important Pauline markings—the author's self-identification, a designation of his intended readers, a claim to apostleship, the customary salutation—it seems that it would have been necessary to include Hebrews *on its own merits.*

» The whole letter contains a sustained appeal in midrashic fashion, employing the argument *a minori ad maius* (Heb. *qal we chomer*), "from the lesser to the greater." We meet this basic argument also in Paul, most strikingly in Rom 5:12-21. Moreover, the transposing of paraenetic sections within a dogmatic body is paralleled in such Pauline writings as Romans (cf. 6:12-14) and Galatians (cf. 4:12-20). Hence neither the argumentative method nor the paraenetic-dogmatic plan of Hebrews can be declared un-Pauline.

» The magnificent prologue in 1:1-4 is perhaps the finest period in the NT.[8] It compares nicely with Paul's eulogy to love in 1 Corinthians 13, a passage that most scholars consider to be a literary masterpiece.[9] Moreover, the preeminence of Christ (1:2-4) finds a conspicuous place in Paul's thinking, as does Christ's creating and sustaining of the cosmos (cf. Eph 1:21; Phil 2:9-10; Col 1:14-19).[10]

---

precedes the Pastorals. See further W. H. P. Hatch, "The Position of Hebrews in the Canon of the New Testament," *HTR* 29 (1936) 133-51.

8 That the *exordium* of Hebrews possibly surpasses that of any other portion of the NT is shown in D. A. Black, "Hebrews 1:1-4: A Study in Discourse Analysis," *Westminster Theological Journal* 49 (1987) 175-94.

9 That Paul was incapable of an elevated style of writing has long been held by NT scholars. Today, however, it is more difficult to assert with unlimited confidence that Paul could not have produced so literary a piece. The epistle to the Philippians, for example, is a highly polished and symmetrical work, containing numerous rhetorical touches (see D. A. Black, "The Discourse Structure of Philippians: A Study in Textlinguistics," *Novum Testamentum* 37 [1995] 16-49). For numerous other examples, see J. D. Harvey, *Listening to the Text: Oral Patterning in Paul's Letters* (Grand Rapids: Baker, 1998).

10 Thus, for example, Heb 1:3 can refer to Christ as God's "impress" (χαρακτήρ, *charaktēr*), a thought substantially repeated in Col 1:15: ὅς ἐστιν εἰκὼν τοῦ θεοῦ (*hos estin eikōn tou theou*). Moreover, the notion of Christ as the instrument of creation (δι' οὗ, *di' hou*) in Heb 1:2 is not without parallel in Paul (cf. Col

» In 1:5-14 the author cites five Psalm passages, the first and last of which are known also to Paul.[11] In Rom 1:4 Paul applies the first passage, Ps 2:7, in the context of Christ's exaltation. The last text, Ps 110:1, is quoted by Paul in 1 Cor 15:25 and alluded to in Rom 8:34; Eph 1:20; Col 3:1. These texts are linked by the adverb "again" (πάλιν, *palin*), which is also used by Paul to join scriptural citations (cf. Rom 15:10-12; 1 Cor 3:20). In 1:8 occurs a direct attribution of deity to Christ that finds explicit parallels in Paul (cf. Rom 9:5; Tit 2:13). Moreover, the author's characteristic method of introducing OT quotations ("he says," or something similar) is paralleled in 1 Cor 6:16; 15:27; 2 Cor 6:2; Gal 3:16; Eph 4:8; 5:14, reflecting the preferred rabbinic formula indicating speech rather than writing. Judging from these parallel formulas in Paul, a *nihil obstat* may still apply with regard to the traditional assumption of Pauline authorship.[12]

» The letter's first exhortation (2:1-4) begins with διὰ τοῦτο (*dia touto*), a construction that Paul uses more than any other NT writer. It also contains the adverb περισσοτέρως (*perissoterōs*), which occurs in the NT only in Heb 2:1; 13:19 and in Paul (10 times). Moreover, the reference in 2:1 to the Christian message as what has been "heard" is paralleled in 2 Tim 1:13; 2:2, while in 2:2 the term "just" (ἔνδικον, *endikon*) appears in only one other place in the NT, where it also refers to fitting justice (Rom 3:8: ὧν τὸ κρίμα ἔνδικον, *hōn to krima endikon*). In addition, the term for "neglect" (ἀμελήσαντες, *amelēsantes*, 2:3) is also found in Paul (1 Tim 4:14). Finally, the use of the verb ἐκφεύγω (*ekpheugō*, 2:3; cf. 12:25) with reference to eschatological punishment is in keeping with Paul's style (cf. Rom 2:3; 1 Thess 5:3).

1:16: ἐν αὐτῷ ἐκτίσθη τὰ πάντα ... τὰ πάντα δι᾽ αὐτοῦ καὶ εἰς αὐτὸν ἔκτισται, *en autō ektisthē ta panta ... ta panta di᾽ autou kai eis auton ektistai*).
11 Paul quotes no less than two dozen Psalms, while Hebrews cites 10.
12 Cf. N. Turner (*A Grammar of New Testament Greek; Vol. 4, Style* [Edinburgh: T & T Clark, 1976] 109): "This impersonal use of 'he says' is quite rabbinical and also Pauline...." That in Hebrews Paul should have more frequently than elsewhere employed λέγει (*legei*), εἶπεν (*eipen*), etc. in introducing OT quotations is altogether consonant with what we may suppose him to have done *when addressing Hebrew Christians.*

» The reference in 2:2-3 to paying more attention to the word spoken by the Lord than to the word spoken by angels finds a striking parallel in Gal 3:19-22 (cf. Col 2:18). One might specifically compare Heb 2:2 (ὁ δι᾽ ἀγγέλων λαληθεὶς λόγος, *ho di᾽ angelōn lalētheis logos*) with Gal 3:19 (ὁ νόμος ... διαταγεὶς δι᾽ ἀγγέλων, *ho nomos ... diatageis di᾽ angelōn*).

» "Confirmed to *us* by those who heard them" (2:3) is no argument against Pauline authorship, inasmuch as Paul had not heard Jesus during the latter's earthly ministry.[13]

» The key salvific term σωτηρία (*sōtēria*, 2:3) is characteristically Pauline (18 times).[14] Likewise, βεβαιόω (*bebaioō*) calls to mind Paul's language about the confirmation of the gospel among his churches (cf. 1 Cor 1:6; Phil 1:7), while the idea of "distributions of the Holy Spirit" (πνεύματος ἁγίου μερισμοῖς, *pneumatos hagiou merismois*) clearly echoes Paul's teaching in 1 Corinthians 12-14.

» In 2:5-18 the eighth Psalm is used in a distinctively Pauline fashion (cf. 1 Cor 15:27), while "crowned with glory and honor" (2:9)[15] re-calls the super-exaltation of Christ in Phil 2:5-11, a passage that may well have come from Paul's hand.[16] Indeed, the whole pericope (2:5-18) evokes an "Adamic" Christology reminiscent of Paul's discussion in Rom 6:2-21; 1 Cor 15:21-22. The solemn term "bore testimony" (διεμαρτύρατο, *diemarturato*), which continues the legal language of 2:1-4, also appears at 1 Tim 5:21; 2 Tim 2:14; 4:1. Moreover, the "glory" (δόξαν, *doxan*) of God's sons (2:10) parallels much of the conceptuality of Paul (cf. Rom 8:17; 1 Cor 15:43; Col 1:27; 3:4;

---

13 It is to be noted that 2:1-4 does not speak of initial impartation of the mes-sage (cf. Gal 1:12) but of confirmation. Thus Paul, though an apostle himself, could refer to specific apostolic traditions that he had received secondhand (cf. 1 Cor 11:2; 15:1). See also Pitts and Walker, "The Authorship of Hebrews," who write (referring to 2:3-4): "So, on the assumption of a Pauline origin for the speech to the Hebrews, Paul seems to be communicating that after having re-ceived his message from Jesus, it was confirmed by the apostles and also through signs and wonders" (p. 182).

14 Luke uses the term 10 times, Peter 5 times.

15 For similar references to "crowning" in Paul, see 1 Cor 9:25; 2 Tim 4:8.

16 For a discussion of the authorship of the Christ hymn of Phil 2:6-11, see D. A. Black, "The Authorship of Philippians 2:6-11: Some Literary-Critical Observations," *Criswell Theological Review* 2 (1988) 269-89.

Phil 3:21), while the religious flavor of ἁγιάζω (*hagiazō*, 2:11) is closely paralleled in 1 Cor 1:2; Eph 5:26; Col 1:22; 1 Thess 5:23. Additionally, "flesh and blood" as an equivalent of human nature is a Pauline expression (cf. 1 Cor 15:50; Gal 1:16; Eph 6:12). Here in 2:14 it occurs in the order αἷμα καὶ σάρξ (*haima kai sarx*), "blood and flesh," an order found elsewhere only in Eph 6:12. Yet another parallel is seen between 2:10 (δι᾽ ὃν ... δι᾽ οὗ τὰ πάντα, *di' hon ... di' hou ta panta*) and Rom 11:36 (ἐξ αὐτοῦ καὶ δι᾽ αὐτοῦ καὶ εἰς αὐτὸν τὰ πάντα, *ex autou kai di' autou kai eis auton ta panta*). Again, the notion of what is "fitting" (ἔπρεπεν, *eprepen*, 2:10) also appears in 1 Tim 2:10; Tit 2:1, while the designation of Christians as "Abraham's seed" (2:16) is paralleled in such Pauline texts as Gal 3:8-9, 29; 4:28-31; Rom 4:1-25. That Christ is reliable and to be trusted (πιστός, *pistos*, 2:17) has affinities in Paul's affirmations of God's reliability in 1 Cor 1:9; 10:13; 2 Cor 2:18; 1 Thess 5:24; 2 Thess 3:3; 2 Tim 2:13, while the accusative construction τὸ πρὸς τὸν θεόν (*to pros ton theon*) in 2:17 is verbally identical to Paul's formulation in Rom 15:17. Finally, the depiction of Christ as our brother (2:11) is paralleled in Rom 8:29, while both the author of Hebrews and Paul view Christ's death as the defeat of evil powers (Heb 2:14; Col 2:15) and as an atoning sacrifice for sin (ἱλάσκομαι, *hilaskomai*, Heb 2:17; ἱλαστήριον, *hilastērion*, Rom 3:25).

» In 3:1 the collocation "holy brothers" (ἀδελφοὶ ἅγιοι, *adelphoi hagioi*) appears elsewhere in the NT only in Col 1:2, while the notion that Christians are "called" by God (κλήσεως ἐπουρανίου μέτοχοι, *klēseōs epouraniou metochoi*) is especially common in Paul (see Rom 1:7; 8:28, 30; Eph 4:14; Col 3:15).[17] The concept of Jesus as "the sent one" (ἀπόστολον, *apostolon*, 3:1) is also affirmed by Paul in Gal 4:4 (ἐξαπέστειλεν ὁ θεὸς τὸν υἱὸν αὐτοῦ, *exapesteilen ho theos ton huion autou*), while the conditional statement "if we hold fast our confidence ..." (3:6) parallels Col 1:23: "if indeed you continue in the faith ...." In addition, the comparison between Moses and Christ is known also to Paul (cf. 1 Cor 10:2), as is the contrast between servant and son (cf. Gal 4:1-7). Finally, the author of Hebrews is

---

17 Significantly, the noun κλῆσις (*klēsis*) appears elsewhere in the NT only in the Pauline corpus and 2 Pet 1:10.

not the only writer to use κατέχω (*katechō*) in paraenetic discourse (3:6), as 1 Cor 11:2; 15:2; 1 Thess 5:21 prove.

» The typology of 3:7-19 contains the key expression ἐπαγγελία (*epangelia*), a word that occurs frequently in the Pauline epistles, especially in the Jewish sections of Romans (8 times) and Galatians (10 times). The Pauline stamp is further discerned in the deterrent example of the wilderness generation (3:12-19; cf. 1 Cor 10:1-13); in the use of "see to it" (βλέπετε, *blepete*, 3:12; cf. 1 Cor 10:18; Col 2:8); in the use of παρακαλέω (*parakaleō*) to introduce concrete exhortations or encouragements (3:13; cf. Rom 12:1; 16:17; 1 Cor 16:15; 2 Cor 10:1; Phil 4:2; 1 Thess 5:11; Eph 4:1; 1 Tim 2:1); in the use of ἑαυτούς (*heautous*, lit., "yourselves") in a reciprocal sense ("one another," 3:13; cf. 1 Thess 5:13; Eph 4:32; Col 3:13, 16); in the phrase ἀπάτη τῆς ἁμαρτίας (*apatē tēs hamartias*, 3:13; cf. 2 Thess 2:10: ἀπάτη ἀδικίας, *apatē adikias*); in the use of ὑπόστασις (*hupostasis*) in the sense of an underlying plan or purpose (3:14; cf. 2 Cor 9:4; 11:17); and in the close association of "disobedience" and "unbelief" (3:18-19; cf. Rom 2:3, 8; 11:20, 23). Moreover, the expression θεὸς ζῶν (*theos zōn*, 3:12) is frequently used by Paul (cf. Rom 2:26; 2 Cor 3:13; 6:16; 1 Thess 1:9; 1 Tim 3:15; 4:10).

» In 4:1-9 numerous Pauline parallels can be cited. The verb ὑστερέω (*hustereō*, 4:1) has the same sense of "fail to reach" or "fall short" in Paul (cf. Rom 3:23; 1 Cor 1:7; 2 Cor 11:5), while the adverb καθάπερ (*kathaper*, "in the same way," 4:2) occurs frequently in the Pauline letters (e.g., Rom 12:4; 1 Cor 10:10; 12:12; 2 Cor 1:14; 1 Thess 3:6, 12) but nowhere else in the NT. The rare expression ὁ λόγος τῆς ἀκοῆς (*ho logos tēs akoēs*, lit., "the word of hearing," 4:2) closely resembles a Pauline idiom for the gospel (1 Thess 2:13, λόγον ἀκοῆς, *logon akoēs*, "word of hearing"), while the use of the particle ἄρα (*ara*) in an initial position (4:9) is no stranger to Paul (cf. Rom 10:17; 1 Cor 15:18). Finally, the notion of the "laying down of the world" (καταβολῆς κόσμου, *katabolēs kosmou*, 4:3) is clearly echoed in Paul (cf. Eph 1:4).

• In 4:12-13 the metaphor of the sword (μάχαιρα, *machaira*)[18] as the word of God seems to betray Paul (cf. Eph 6:17), while the notion of the word probing the innermost recesses of the heart and bring-

---

18 In other NT metaphorical texts, ῥομφαία (*rhomphaia*) is used.

8

ing subconscious motives to light finds a strong parallel in Paul's reference to the day when the Lord "will both bring to light the hidden things of darkness and manifest the counsels of the heart" (1 Cor 4:5). Moreover, the idea that the word is "active" (ἐνεργής, energēs) is paralleled in 1 Thess 2:13, where the word of God is said to ἐνεργεῖται ἐν ὑμῖν τοῖς πιστεύουσιν (energeitai en humin tois pisteuousin; see 1 Cor 1:18; 2 Cor 6:7 for Paul's theology of the word of God as power). Finally, the distinction between ψυχή (psuchē) and πνεῦμα (pneuma) is also made in 1 Thess 5:23 (cf. 1 Cor 15:44-46), while the notion that nothing is hidden from God finds its closest NT parallels in Rom 8:27; 1 Cor 4:5; 1 Thess 2:4.

» The final verses of chapter 4 (4:14-16) contain at least two Pauline words (ὁμολογία, homologia, and ἀσθένεια, astheneia),[19] while the exhortation to "approach the throne of grace" recalls Rom 5:2 (τὴν προσαγωγὴν ἐσχήκαμεν τῇ πίστει εἰς τὴν χάριν ταύτην, tēn prosagōgēn eschēkamen tē pistei eis tēn charin tautēn; cf. Eph 2:18; 3:12). Moreover, the use of litotes ("we do not have a high priest who is not able ...") is paralleled in Paul (e.g., 1 Thess 4:13: "We do not want you not to know ..."), as is the use of the participle ἔχοντες (echontes) followed by a hortatory subjunctive (e.g., 2 Cor 7:1). Again, the notion of Christ's "passage through heaven" (διεληλυθότα τοὺς οὐρανούς, dielēluthota tous ouranous) is also found in Paul (cf. Eph 4:10), while the picture of Christ sympathizing with human "weaknesses" (ἀσθενείαις, astheneiais) is developed in Paul as well (cf. Rom 6:19; 1 Cor 15:43; Gal 4:13).[20] Finally, the affirmation that Christ was "without sin" (χωρὶς ἁμαρτίας, chōris hamartias) is also made by Paul in 2 Cor 5:21, while "mercy" (ἔλεος, eleos) and "grace" (χάρις, charis) are also collocated in the Pastoral Epistles (1 Tim 1:2; 2 Tim 1:2; Tit 1:4).

---

19 The noun ὁμολογία (homologia) occurs only 6 times in the NT, 3 times in Paul and 3 times in Hebrews. Likewise, "weakness" is a Pauline concept. For a detailed discussion of ἀσθένεια (astheneia) and related terms in Paul, see D. A. Black, *Paul, Apostle of Weakness: Astheneia and its Cognates in the Pauline Literature* (Rev. ed.; Eugene, OR: Pickwick, 2012).
20 Cf. D. A. Black, "*Paulus Infirmus*: The Pauline Concept of Weakness," *Grace Theological Journal* 5 (1984) 77-93.

» The section of Hebrews beginning in 5:1 that deals with the sacerdotal work of Christ—a subject treated nowhere else in the NT—naturally shows fewer parallels with the Pauline writings.[21] Yet parallels do exist. Just as the author of Hebrews had to rebuke his readers for their dullness of heart (5:11-14), so Paul declared that he could not speak the wisdom of God to the Corinthians because they were infants in Christ, incapable of solid food (1 Cor 3:1-3). The parallel between these two passages is not limited to vocabulary (νήπιος, *nēpios*, γάλα, *gala*, τέλειος, *teleios*, στοιχεῖον, *stoicheion*),[22] but involves conceptual affinities as well. For example, the image of γεγυμνασμένα (*gegumnasmena*, 5:14) points to 1 Tim 4:7 (γύμναζε δὲ σεαυτὸν πρὸς εὐσέβειαν, *gumnaze de seauton pros eusebeian*), while the phrase πρὸς διάκρισιν καλοῦ τε καὶ κακοῦ (*pros diakrisin kalou te kai kakou*) finds its closest NT parallels in Rom 7:21 (τῷ θέλοντι ἐμοὶ ποιεῖν τὸ καλόν, ὅτι ἐμοὶ τὸ καλὸν παράκειται, *tō thelonti emoi poiein to kalon, hoti emoi to kalon parakeitai*) and Rom 12:21 (μὴ νικῶ ὑπὸ τοῦ κακοῦ ἀλλὰ νίκα ἐν τῷ ἀγαθῷ τὸ κακόν, *mē nikō hupo tou kakou alla nika en tō agathō to kakon*). Moreover, the term "obedience" (ὑπακοή, *hupakoē*) that appears only here in Hebrews (5:8) is common in Paul, especially in Romans (cf. 1:5; 5:9; 6:16; 15:18; 16:19, 26).

» In 6:1-3 Pauline parallels exist with τελειότης (*teleiotēs*), θεμέλιος (*themelios*), νεκρὰ ἔργα (*nekra erga*), and ἐάνπερ ἐπιτρέπῃ ὁ θεός (*eanper epitrepē ho theos*). The first expression is found only

21 One of the chief arguments against the Pauline authorship of our epistle is the feeling that the author of the Galatian, Corinthian, and Roman letters could not have adapted himself as a writer to the situation with which Πρὸς Ἑβραίους (*Pros Hēbraious*) deals. But this is to impose a completely unwarranted limitation to Paul's intelligence, versatility, and originality as an author. He whose policy was to be "all things to all people" (1 Cor 9:22-24) was surely not incapable of confronting the erring readers of this letter with the finality of Christ and Christianity. Perhaps in Hebrews we hear Paul the Rabbi more clearly than in his other writings.

22 Each of these terms has a Pauline flavor. Outside of the Gospels, νήπιος (*nēpios*) is a distinctly Pauline word; γάλα (*gala*) occurs twice in Paul, twice in Hebrews, and once in 1 Peter; τέλειος (*teleios*) occurs 3 times in the Gospels, 8 times in Paul, twice in Hebrews, 5 times in James, and once in 1 John; στοιχεῖον (*stoicheion*) occurs 4 times in Paul, once in Hebrews, and twice in 2 Peter.

here and in Col 3:14; the second is used in the figurative sense only by Luke (twice), Paul (7 times), and the author of Hebrews (twice); the idea of "dead works" is closest to the idea of James 2:26 but is not far from the concept of Eph 2:1, 5; Col 2:13; and the words "if God permits" admit verbal comparison only with 1 Cor 16:7 (ἐὰν ὁ κύριος ἐπιτρέψῃ, *ean ho kurios epitrepsē*).[23] Moreover, the concept of "laying on of hands" is not unknown to Paul (cf. 1 Tim 4:14; 5:22, 2 Tim 1:6).

» In the following verses (6:4-8) Pauline affinities are seen in the usage of φωτίζω (*phōtizō*, 4 times in Paul, once in Luke), while the cognate φωτισμός (*phōtismos*) occurs only in 2 Cor 4:4, 6. Although the noun μέτοχος (*metochos*) is absent from the Pauline corpus, its corresponding verbal form μετέχω (*metechō*) is peculiar to 1 Corinthians (5 times) and Hebrews (3 times). Again, while ἀνακαινίζω (*anakainizō*) occurs only in Heb 6:6, its cognates are exclusively Pauline (for ἀνακαινόω, *anakainoō*, see 2 Cor 4:16 and Col 3:10; for ἀνακαίνωσις, *anakainōsis*, see Rom 12:2 and Tit 3:5). The agricultural imagery in 6:7-8 is echoed in Pauline thought (cf. 2 Cor 3:6, 9), as is the γεωργ- (*geōrg-*) root (cf. 1 Cor 3:9; 2 Tim 2:6). Finally, the sense of τέλος (*telos*) as an unwelcome fate is also found in 2 Cor 11:15; Phil 3:19, while the adjective ἀδόκιμος (*adokimos*) is paralleled in the NT only in Paul (cf. Rom 1:28; 1 Cor 9:27; 2 Cor 13:5, 6, 7; 2 Tim 3:8; Tit 1:16).

» In 6:9-12 we find significant Pauline parallels. The denial that God is ἄδικος (*adikos*, 6:10) is paralleled in Rom 3:5 (ἄδικος ὁ θεός, *adikos ho theos*); the idea that love must be "manifested" (ἐνεδείξασθε, *enedeixasthe*, 6:10) is also found in 2 Cor 8:24; Tit 2:10; 3:2; the perfect tense form of πείθω (*peithō*) occurs only here (6:9) and in Paul (cf. Rom 8:38; 15:14; 2 Tim 1:5, 12);[24] the triad faith-hope-love (6:10-12) is demonstrably Pauline (cf. 1 Cor 13:13; Col 1:4-5; Eph

---

23 For other instances of *Deo volente* in Paul, see Rom 1:10; 1 Cor 4:19.
24 It is noteworthy that this expression of confidence (πεπείσμεθα, *pepeismetha*), a conventional rhetorical device, is found only in Hebrews and Paul. See S. N. Olson, "Pauline Expressions of Confidence in His Addressees," *CBQ* 47 (1985) 282-95.

1:15, 18; 1 Thess 1:3);[25] the idea of "service to the saints" (6:10) is paralleled in Rom 15:25; 2 Cor 9:1; the notion that God judges each person according to works (6:10) is strongly echoed in Paul (cf. Gal 6:4; Rom 2:6-7; 1 Cor 3:13-15); the term ἐπιθυμέω (*epithumeō*) for "strong desire" is paralleled in Rom 13:9; 1 Tim 3:1; and the term πληροφορία (*plērophoria*, 6:11) also occurs in Col 2:2; 1 Thess 1:5. Finally, μιμητής (*mimētēs*, 6:12) is otherwise exclusively Paul's (1 Cor 4:6; 11:1; Eph 5:1; 1 Thess 1:6; 2:14).

» In the final section of chapter 6 (verses 13-20) the example of Abraham recalls Romans 4:1-25 and Gal 3:16-18, while the phrase ἀδύνατον ψεύσασθαι τὸν θεόν (*adunaton pseusasthai ton theon*, 6:18) finds a unique parallel in Paul's expression ὁ ἀψευδὴς θεός (*ho apseudēs theos*, Tit 1:2). Moreover, in the NT the verb ἐπιτυγχάνω (*epitunchanō*) appears only here (6:15) and at Rom 11:7; James 4:2. Finally, the use of βεβαίωσις/βέβαιος (*bebaiōsis/bebaios*, 6:16, 19) has a clear Pauline ring to it (cf. Phil 1:7; Rom 4:6; 2 Cor 1:6).

» In the discussion of the character, dignity, and efficacy of the high-priesthood of Christ in 7:1-10:18, there is a certain presumption of Paulinity in the use of μερίζω (*merizō*, 7:2) to mean "apportion" (cf. Rom 12:3; 2 Cor 10:13); in the phrase ἐξ ἀνάγκης (*ex anankēs*, 7:12), which elsewhere occurs only in 2 Cor 9:7; in the use of the correlative πηλίκος (*pēlikos*), which is found only here (7:14) and in Gal 6:11; in the use of προσέχω (*prosechō*, 7:13) in the sense "be occupied with" (cf. 1 Tim 3:8; 4:1, 13); in the use of the adjective πρόδηλον (*prodēlon*, 7:14), which appears elsewhere only in 1 Tim 5:24-25; in the use of σαρκίνης (*sarkinēs*, 7:16), which is otherwise used in the NT only in Paul (cf. Rom 7:14; 1 Cor 3:1; 2 Cor 3:3); in the reference in 7:25 to Christ's constant intercessory agency (πάντοτε ζῶν εἰς τὸ ἐντυγχάνειν, *pantote zōn eis to entunchanein*; cf. Rom 8:34: ὃς καὶ ἐντυγχάνει ὑπὲρ ἡμῶν, *hos kai entunchanei huper hēmōn*); in the use of κτίσις (*ktisis*, 9:11) for the whole creation (cf. Rom 1:25; 8:19-22; Col 1:15, 23); in the reference to πνεῦμα (*pneuma*, 9:14) in formulas relating to the exaltation of Christ (cf. Rom 1:4; 1 Cor 15:45; 1 Tim 3:16); in the use of ἄφεσις (*aphesis*, 9:22) for the forgiveness of sins (cf. Eph 1:7; Col 1:14); in

---

25 Of special significance is 1 Thess 1:3, where Paul links the "work of faith," the "toil of love," and the "endurance of hope" as evidences of genuine salvation.

the use of νυνὶ δέ (*nuni de*), which is found only in Hebrews (9:26) and Paul (cf., e.g., Rom 3:21; 1 Cor 15:20; Col 1:22); in the reference in 9:26 to Christ's "once and for all" (ἅπαξ, *hapax*) suffering (cf. Rom 6:10: τῇ ἁμαρτίᾳ ἀπέθανεν ἐφάπαξ, *tē hamartia apethanen ephapax*); in the eschatological use of ἀποδέχομαι (*apodechomai*, 9:28; cf. Rom 8:19, 23, 25; 1 Cor 1:7; Gal 5:5; Phil 3:30); in the comparison in 10:1 of the Mosaic dispensation with the Christian as a "shadow" to the substance (σκιὰν γὰρ ἔχων ὁ νόμος τῶν μελλόντων, *skian gar echōn ho nomos tōn mellontōn*; cf. Col 2:17: ἅ ἐστι σκιὰ τῶν μελλόντων, *ha esti skia tōn mellontōn*); in the collocation of παύω (*pauō*) + participle (10:2; cf. Eph 1:16; Col 1:9); in the expression "to take away sins" (ἀφαιρεῖν ἁμαρτίας, *aphairein hamartias*, 10:4), which appears elsewhere in the NT only in the citation of Isa 27:9 at Rom 11:27; in the connection between the will of God and sanctification (10:10; cf. 1 Thess 4:3); in the reference to the salvific import of Christ's "body" (σῶμα, *sōma*), 10:10; cf. Rom 7:4; Col 1:22); in the use of the verb λειτουργέω (*leitourgeō*), which in the NT appears only here (10:11) and in Rom 15:27; Acts 13:2; in the adverbial use of τὸ λοιπόν (*to loipon*, 10:13), which is a Pauline expression (cf. 2 Thess 3:1; Phil 3:1; 4:8; 1 Cor 7:29; Eph 6:10 [τοῦ λοιποῦ, *tou loipou*]); in the phrase ἀσθενὲς καὶ ἀνωφελές (*asthenes kai anōpheles*) to describe the law (7:18; cf. Rom 8:3; Gal 4:9);[26] in the reference to tabernacle-worship as a shadow of the heavenly things (8:5; cf. Col 2:17); in the distinction between the old and new covenants (8:7-13; cf. 2 Cor 3:6-14); in the description of Christ's intercession for us (7:25; cf. Rom 8:34); and in the description of Christ's death as a θυσία (*thusia*) and a προσφορά (*prosphora*, 10:5; cf. προσφορὰν καὶ θυσίαν, *prosphoran kai thusian* in Eph 5:2). In addition, the language of "cleansing" (καθαρίζω, *katharizō*; 9:14, 22, 23; 10:2) is reminiscent of 2 Cor 7:1 and Eph 5:26.

» The concluding portion of Hebrews (10:19-13:17) also admits of numerous Pauline parallels. The affirmation that God is πιστός (*pistos*, 10:23) is commonplace in Paul (cf. 1 Thess 5:24; 2 Thess 3:3; 1 Cor 1:9; 10:13; 2 Cor 1:18). The noun ἐπίγνωσις (*epignōsis*), found only here in Hebrews (10:26), is frequent in Paul (15 times).

---

26 On Gal 4:9 see D. A. Black, "Weakness Language in Galatians," *Grace Theological Journal* 4 (1983) 15-36.

Similar uses of ἀλήθεια (*alētheia*) for the Christian faith (10:26) occur at Gal 5:7; Eph 1:13; 2 Thess 2:12; 2 Tim 2:15. On the use of κομίζω (*komizō*, 10:36) for eschatological acquisitions, see 2 Cor 5:10; Eph 6:8; Col 3:25. On the notion of *creatio ex nihilo* (11:3), see Rom 4:17. On the contrast between what is seen and what is unseen (11:3), see Rom 8:24-25; 1 Cor 13:12; 2 Cor 4:18. The declaration that "without faith it is impossible to please God" (11:6) is suggestive of Paul (cf. Rom 10:14). The relation between faith and righteousness (11:7) has a loud Pauline ring to it (cf. Rom 3:22; 4:5, 9, 11, 13; 9:30; 10:4, 6; Phil 3:9). The description of Abraham as νενεκρωμένου (*nenekrōmenou*, 11:12) recalls Paul's discussion in Rom 4:19 (νενεκρωμένον, *nenekrōmenon*). On "the reproach of Christ" (11:26; cf. 13:13), see Rom 15:3. The term for "discipliners" (παιδευτάς, *paideutas*, 12:9) appears elsewhere in the NT only at Rom 2:20. That the readers are to "pursue peace with all" (12:14) recalls Paul's use of the same motif (cf. Rom 12:18; 1 Thess 5:13; 2 Cor 13:11). The adjective βέβηλος (*bebēlos*, "profane," 12:16) is a Pauline term (cf. 1 Tim 1:9; 4:7; 6:20; 2 Tim 2:16). The command to "remember" (μνημονεύετε, *mnēmoneuete*, 13:7) is frequent in the Pauline literature (cf. 1 Thess 1:3; 2:9; Col 4:18; Eph 2:11; 2 Tim 2:8). The glorious "outcome" (ἔκβασιν, *ekbasin*) of the leaders (13:7) finds its only verbal parallel in 1 Cor 10:13 (ἔκβασιν, *ekbasin*). The clause "that he might sanctify the people through his own blood" (13:12) combines two ideas found in Eph 1:7 ("through his blood") and 5:26 ("that he might sanctify her"). The rare particle τοίνυν (*toinun*, 13:13) occurs in the NT only here and in 1 Cor 9:26; Luke 20:25. Moreover, the Pauline triad faith-hope-love reappears in 10:19-25, while the quotation from Deut 32:35 in Heb 10:30 is reproduced in identical form in Rom 12:19.[27] The image contained in θεατριζόμενοι (*theatrizomenoi*, 10:33) recalls Paul's own "theatrical" exposure in 1 Cor 4:9 (ὅτι θέατρον ἐγενήθημεν, *hoti theatron egenēthēmen*), while the citation in 10:38 of Hab 2:4 is peculiar to the Apostle to the Gentiles (Rom 1:17; Gal 3:11). The description of Abraham's faith in 11:8-10 conveys the same idea as that in Romans 4, while the exhortation to "run with endurance" (12:1)

---

27 This is all the more striking in that the citation reproduces neither the words of the Hebrew text nor those of the Septuagint.

recalls the athletic imagery so characteristic of Paul, who uses ἀγών (*agōn*) metaphorically in Phil 1:30; Col 2:1; 1 Thess 2:2; 1 Tim 6:12; 2 Tim 4:7. Finally, the idea of Jesus as a μεσίτης (*mesitēs*, 12:24; cf. 8:6; 9:15) clearly belongs to the theology of Paul (cf. 1 Tim 2:5).

» The parallels between the epilogue of Hebrews (13:18-25) and the Pauline epistles are both numerous and striking. The entire passage bears the seal of the great apostle. The exhortation to "pray for us" (cf. 1 Thess 5:25; 2 Thess 3:1); the concept of συνείδησις (*suneidēsis*, see esp. Rom 9:1; 2 Cor 1:12; 2 Tim 1:3); the apostolic appeal to ὁ θεὸς τῆς εἰρήνης (*ho theos tēs eirēnēs*, cf. Rom 15:33; 16:20; 1 Cor 14:33; 16:11; 2 Cor 13:11; Phil 4:9; 1 Thess 5:23); the reference to ὁ ἀναγωγὼν ἐκ νεκρῶν (*ho anagōgōn ek nekrōn*, cf. Rom 10:7); the combination of τὸν κύριον ἡμῶν ᾿Ιησοῦν (*ton kurion hēmōn Iēsoun*, cf. 1 Cor 16:23); the word of apology couched in the form of a plea for indulgence (cf. Rom 15:15; 2 Cor 11:1); the mention of travel plans (cf. Rom 15:22-29); the concluding salutations (cf. Rom 16:3-16; 1 Cor 16:20; 2 Cor 13:12; Phil 4:21; 1 Thess 5:26; 2 Tim 4:19); the words ἡ χάρις μετὰ πάντων ὑμῶν (*hē charis meta pantōn humōn*, cf. Rom 16:20; 2 Cor 13:13; Gal 6:18; Eph 6:24; Phil 4:23; Col 4:18; 1 Thess 5:28; 2 Thess 3:18; 1 Tim 6:21; Phm 25)—all have no more likely an author than Paul and help to confirm the tradition that the apostle wrote our epistle, confirmation and not proof being all that coincidences of phraseology can offer.[28]

THE STYLE OF HEBREWS AND THE QUESTION OF AUTHORSHIP

Let us now turn our attention more particularly to matters of style. In an essay published in *Filologia Neotestamentaria*,[29] I discussed the literary style of Hebrews as seen in four primary areas: euphony, diction, syntax, and mode of argumentation. An interesting and related matter of interpretation is the bearing the examples of literary artistry discussed

28 Of special interest is the term συνείδησις (*suneidēsis*), which occurs only twice in Acts, 3 times in 1 Peter, 4 times in Hebrews, but 20 times in Paul. Moreover, the adjective εὐάρεστος (*euarestos*) appears only here (13:21) and in the Pauline corpus (cf. Rom 12:2; 14:18; 2 Cor 5:9; Eph 5:10; Phil 4:18; Col 3:20; Tit 2:9).

29 D. A. Black, "Literary Artistry in the Epistle to the Hebrews," *FN* 7 (1994) 43-52.

in that essay may have on the question of the letter's authorship. If we examine the question of euphony, not only are alliteration, paronomasia, and assonance regular features of Hebrews, but they also find a sizable home in the Pauline Corpus.[30] It is a pleasure to read even an abbreviated list of these literary adornments. In Paul's earliest writing, 1 Thessalonians, we have such examples as παράκλησις πλάνης (*paraklēsis planēs*) in 2:3, παρακαλοῦντες παραμυθούμενοι περιπατεῖν (*parakalountes paramuthoumenoi peripatein*) in 2:11, and ὁλοτελεῖς ὁλόκληρον (*holoteleis holoklēron*) in 5:23. The Great Epistles furnish so many examples that we can almost consider euphony a hallmark of these letters. Instances of rhetorical flourishes include the following:

» Rom 1:29-31: ἀδικία (*adikia*), πονηρία (*ponēria*), πλεονεξία (*pleonexia*), κακία (*kakia*), φθόνου φόνου (*phthonou phonou*), ἀσυνέτους ἀσυνθέτους (*asunetous asunthetous*)

» Rom 12:3: μὴ ὑπερφρονεῖν παρ᾽ ὃ δεῖ φρονεῖν ἀλλὰ φρονεῖν εἰς τὸ σωφρονεῖν (*mē huperphronein par' ho dei phronein alla phronein eis to sōphronein*)

» Rom 12:15: χαίρειν μετὰ χαιρόντων, κλαίειν μετὰ κλαιόντων (*chairein meta chairontōn, klaiein meta klaiontōn*)

» 1 Cor 11:31: εἰ δὲ ἑαυτοὺς διεκρίνομεν, οὐκ ἂν ἐκρινόμεθα (*ei de heautous diekrinomen, ouk an ekrinometha*)

» 1 Cor 14:3: παράκλησιν καὶ παραμυθίαν (*paraklēsin kai paramuthian*)

» 2 Cor 1:13: ἃ ἀναγινώσκετε ἢ καὶ ἐπιγινώσκετε (*ha anaginōskete ē kai epiginōskete*)

» 2 Cor 3:2: γινωσκομένη καὶ ἀναγινωσκομένη (*ginōskomenē kai anaginōskomenē*)

» 2 Cor 4:8: ἀπορούμενοι ἀλλ᾽ οὐκ ἐξαπορούμενοι (*aporoumenoi all' ouk exaporoumenoi*)

From the Captivity and Pastoral Epistles we find:

» Eph 3:6: συγκληρονόμα καὶ σύσσωμα καὶ συμμέτοχα (*sunklēronoma kai sussōma kai summetocha*)

---

30 Elsewhere I have sought to examine the obvious literary qualities of certain Pauline texts; see D. A. Black, "The Pauline Love Command: Structure, Style, and Ethics in Romans 12:9-21," *FN* 2 (1989) 3-22; and "Paul and Christian Unity: A Formal Analysis of Philippians 2:1-4," *JETS* 28 (1985) 299-308.

» Phil 3:2-3: κατατομήν περιτομή (*katatomēn peritomē*)
» 1 Tim 1:17: ἀφθάρτῳ ἀοράτῳ μόνῳ θεῷ (*aphthartō aoratō monō theō*)
» 1 Tim 4:1: πίστεως προσέχοντες πνεύμασιν πλάνοις (*pisteōs prosechontes pneumasin planois*)
» 2 Tim 3:2: φίλαυτοι φιλάργυροι ἀχάριστοι ἀνόσιοι (*philautoi philarguroi acharistoi anosioi*)
» 2 Tim 3:4: φιλήδονοι φιλόθεοι (*philēdonoi philotheoi*)

This list could easily be augmented.

As far as diction goes, the *argumentum ad quantitatum* (argument based on quantity) does little to disprove Pauline authorship, since the extensiveness of Paul's vocabulary shows the apostle to have had a large storehouse of words. Assuming the Pauline authorship of the Pastorals, the writer of the Pauline corpus has over 600 words in common with Hebrews and about the same number not found elsewhere in the NT. Concerning the matter of *hapax legomena* (words occurring only once) found in Hebrews, we may say that none of them can be reasonably marked as un-Pauline. For example, adjectives in alpha-privative found in Hebrews (e.g., ἀπαράβατος, *aparabatos*), ἀκατάλυτος (*akatalutos*), ἀμετάθετος (*ametathetos*) are paralleled in such Pauline formulations as ἀπαρασκεύατος (*aparaskeuatos*), ἀκατακάλυπτος (*akatakaluptos*), and ἀμετακίνητος (*ametakinētos*). Nor are nouns in -σις (*-sis*), so frequent in Hebrews (e.g., ἀθέτησις, *athetēsis*, ἄθλησις, *athlēsis*, διόρθωσις, *diorthōsis*), unknown in the Paulines (e.g., ἀνακαίνωσις, *anakainōsis*, ἀπέκδυσις, *apekdusis*).

One must also take into account the relatively large number of words in Hebrews that are otherwise exclusively Pauline. The following is but a partial listing:

ἁγιότης (*hagiotēs*), ἀγών (*agōn*), ἀδόκιμος (*adokimos*), ἀνυπότακτος (*anupotaktos*), ἀόρατος (*aoratos*), ἀφιλάργυρος (*aphilarguros*), ἀφοράω (*aphoraō*), βεβαίωσις (*bebaiōsis*), διάκρισις (*diakrisis*), δουλεία (*douleia*), ἔκβασις (*ekbasis*), ἔνδικος (*endikos*), εὐάρεστος (*euarestos*), θαρρέω (*tharreō*), καύκημα (*kaukēma*), κοσμικός (*kosmikos*), λειτουργός (*leitourgos*), μεσίτης (*mesitēs*), μιμητής (*mimētēs*), οἰκτιρμός (*oiktirmos*), παιδευτής (*paideutēs*), παράβασις (*parabasis*), παρακοή (*parakoē*), πλάξ (*plax*), πόμα (*poma*), τελειωτής (*teleiōtēs*), τοιγαροῦν (*toigaroun*), ὑπόστασις (*hupostasis*), φιλοξενία (*philoxenia*), φράσσω (*phrassō*)

These words are all the more interesting in that they are comparatively rare but characteristically Pauline. The unusual triple particle τοιγαροῦν (*toigaroun*), for example, occurs only in Hebrews and 1 Thess 4:8. The term τελειωτής (*teleiōtēs*, 6:1) is limited to Hebrews and Col 3:14. The noun ἀγών (*agōn*, 12:2) is entirely Paul's (Phil 1:30; Col 2:1; 1 Thess 2:2; 1 Tim 6:12; 2 Tim 4:7). The verb θαρρέω (*tharreō*) is found in 13:6 and elsewhere only in 2 Corinthians. The adjective ἀφιλάργυρος (*aphilarguros*) occurs only in Hebrews (13:5) and in 1 Tim 3:3.

Then there are terms found in Hebrews that are characteristically, though not exclusively, Pauline. Although many of these terms were discussed earlier in this book, it may be helpful here to remind the reader of their cumulative effect. The noun σωτηρία (*sōtēria*) is a Pauline word, as is the term ἀσθένεια (*astheneia*) in a moral sense. The perfect of πείθω (*peithō*) occurs only in Hebrews and in Rom 8:38; 15:14; 2 Tim 1:5, 12. The noun θεμέλιος (*themelios*) in the figurative sense is peculiar to Luke (2 times), the Pauline epistles (7 times), and Hebrews. The term στοιχεῖον (*stoicheion*) in its metaphorical sense is otherwise entirely Pauline. In the contrast between "milk" and "meat" we recognize Pauline affinities. The connection διὰ τοῦτο (*dia touto*) is more frequent in the Pauline letters than in any other writings of the NT. The verb ἀνακαινίζω (*anakainizō*) is peculiar to Hebrews, but ἀνακαινόω (*anakainoō*, 2 Cor 4:16; Col 3:10) and ἀνακαίνωσις (*anakainōsis*, Rom 12:2; Tit 3:5) are exclusively Pauline. The triad faith-hope-love (cf. 6:9-13; 10:19-25) is Paul's. The "weakness of the law" (7:18) is a familiar thought to Paul (Rom 8:3). Only the author of Hebrews (9:26; 10:10, 12) and Paul (Eph 5:2) call Christ's death a θυσία (*thusia*) and a προσφορά (*prosphora*). Outside of the Gospels and Hebrews the term δέσμιος (*desmios*) describes only Paul. Only Hebrews (13:2) and Paul (Rom 12:13) put φιλαδελφία (*philadelphia*) and φιλονεξία (*philonexia*) side by side.

A careful reading of the Pauline epistles will also reveal a remarkable number of images and metaphors, many of them analogous to those found in Hebrews. Although it is possible to explain these coincidences by supposing either that our author derived his language from the writings of Paul or that both drew from some common source, it is just as possible that they are directly traceable to the mind of Paul. The term παιδεία (*paideia*) in the moral sense is used only by the author of Hebrews and Paul (cf. Eph 6:4; 2 Tim 3:16). The term κοίτη (*koitē*) in its sexual sense is found only in Hebrews and Rom 9:10; 13:13. The metaphorical use of ῥίζα (*rhiza*) fits in well with Paul's teaching in Rom 11:16-18; Eph 3:17; Col 2:7; 1 Tim 6:10. The "two-edged sword" of Heb 4:12 reminds one of Paul's "sword of the Spirit" in Eph 6:17. Nautical metaphors are not limited to Hebrews but are also found in Paul (cf. Eph 4:14; 1 Tim 1:19), as are expressions drawn from religion (cf. Rom 9:33; 11:16; Gal 4:26). Architectural images similar to those found in Hebrews have inspired numerous Pauline passages (cf. 1 Cor 3:9-10; Eph 2:20; 4:16). Finally, athletic images such as γυμνάζω (*gumnazō*) and τρέχω (*trechō*) seem to cry "I am of Paul" (cf. 1 Cor 9:24-26; Gal 2:2; 5:7; Phil 2:16; 1 Tim 4:7).

Concerning the letter's syntax and phraseology, Hebrews's penchant for anarthrous nouns finds a parallel in Paul's υἱὸς θεοῦ (*huios theou*, Rom 1:4) and ἄνθρωπος Χριστὸς Ἰησοῦς (*anthrōpos Christos Iēsous*, 1 Tim 2:5). The anarthrous σταυρός (*stauros*) of Heb 12:2 finds an exact parallel in Phil 2:8. Hyperbaton, though rare in Paul, is not altogether lacking, as 1 Thess 2:13 proves: παραλαβόντες λόγον ἀκοῆς (παρ᾽ ἡμῶν) τοῦ θεοῦ (*paralabontes logon akoēs [par' hēmōn] tou theou*, cf. Gal 2:6; 6:11). The genitive absolutes of Hebrews find numerous parallels in Paul's letters (e.g., 5 in Romans, 3 in 1 Corinthians, 5 in 2 Corinthians). A famous example of a boxed/embedded genitive absolute occurs in 1 Cor 5:3-5:

ἤδη κέκρικα ὡς παρὼν τὸν οὕτως τοῦτο κατεργασάμενον (ἐν τῷ ὀνόματι τοῦ κυρίου ἡμῶν Ἰησοῦ συναχθέντων ὑμῶν καὶ τοῦ ἐμοῦ πνεύματος σὺν τῇ δυνάμει τοῦ κυρίου ἡμῶν Ἰησοῦ) παραδοῦναι τὸν τοιοῦτον τῷ Σατανᾷ (*ēdē kekrika hōs parōn ton houtōs touto katergasamenon [en tō onomati tou kuriou hēmōn Iēsou sunachthentōn humōn kai tou emou pneumatos sun tē dunamei tou kuriou hēmōn Iēsou] paradounai ton toiouton tō Satana*).

Under the heading of periodism, we cannot deny to Paul many finely balanced sentences—1 Thess 1:2-7; 2 Thess 2:3-12; 1 Cor 1:4-8;

19

2 Cor 1:3-7; Rom 2:17-23, to name but a few. These sentences may not attain the full periodic structure of Hebrews, but if Πρὸς Ἑβραίους (*Pros Hebraious*) is Pauline, then perhaps we may owe its artistry in this instance to the hand of an amanuensis (or secretary). The participles μέν...δέ (*men ... de*) are fairly frequent in Paul, especially in 1 Corinthians, where contrast plays an important role. In fact, the instances in 1 Corinthians alone are slightly more numerous than those in Hebrews, which shows that antithesis is not alien to the thought of the Apostle to the Gentiles.

As for oratorical imperatives, we need only point to Gal 3:3, 21; 4:15; 5:7; 6:11, or to the Pauline "Be imitators of me" in 1 Cor 11:1 and Phil 3:17. Nor are the Pauline letters devoid of dramatic questions. Single questions occur in Rom 7:7; Gal 4:9, 21, 30; 5:7, 11; double questions in Rom 2:3, 4; 4:1, 3; 6:15, 16; 7:7; Gal 4:15, 16; triple in Rom 3:1-3, 29-31; quadruple in Rom 6:1-3; quintuple in Rom 2:21-23; 3:5-8; sextuple in Gal 3:1-6; and septuple in Rom 8:31-35. We may also compare the manner in which these questions are introduced in Hebrews and the Paulines:

		Hebrews	Paul
τίς	(*tis*)	frequently	frequently
τί ἔτι	(*ti eti*)	11:32	Rom 3:7; Gal 5:11
πῶς	(*pōs*)	2:3	frequently
οὐχί	(*ouchi*)	1:14	Rom 3:29; 1 Cor (frequently)
πόσῳ μᾶλλον	(*posō mallon*)	9:14	Rom 11:12, 24

Participial and adjectival ternaries (triads) find parallels in 1 Thess 5:12 (κοπιῶντας ... προϊσταμένους...νουθετοῦντας, *kopiōntas ... proistamenous ... nouthetountas*) and Col 1:22 (ἁγίους καὶ ἀμώμους καὶ ἀνεγκλήτους, *hagious kai amōmous kai anenklētous*). 1 Thessalonians has a total of nine ternaries, while 2 Thessalonians has at least three. As far as anaphora is concerned, we may note the repetition of ἐάν (*ean*) in 1 Cor 13:1-3, of ἐν (*en*), διά (*dia*), and ὡς (*hōs*) in 2 Cor 6:4-7, and of τούτου χάριν (*toutou charin*) at the beginning of the main clauses in Eph 3:1-21.

As to the letter's method of composition and argumentation,[31] the chiastic arrangement of words and even larger units of discourse has also left traces in the Pauline corpus. An excellent example of Pauline chiasm is offered in the Christ-hymn of Phil 2:6-11, where the exact center is the double affirmation of Christ's death: μεχρὶ θανάτου/θανάτου δὲ σταυροῦ (*mechri thanatou/thanatou de staurou*). Another noteworthy example of Pauline chiasm is 1 Corinthians 12-14, where A and A' pivot around the central theme B:

A = Varieties of spiritual gifts (12:1-30)
  B = Love as the highest gift (12:31-14:1b)
A'= Varieties of spiritual gifts: tongues and prophecy (14:1c-40)

Here the theme of the central section is highlighted by an inclusio: "earnestly desire the highest gifts" (12:31)/ "earnestly desire spiritual gifts" (14:1b). To this may be added the well-ordered composition and fine rhythm of 1 Corinthians 13, a literary masterpiece that, like Hebrews, shows a marked tendency towards Hellenistic symmetry.

A final example of chiasm in Paul can be draw from the central section of Philippians (1:12-2:30):

A = News about Paul's imprisonment (1:12-26)
  B = Instructions for the church (1:27-2:18)
A'= News about Paul's companions (2:19-30)

The passage is also carefully arranged according to the principle of inclusio:

Subsection	Inclusio	
1:12-26	1:12	προκοπήν (*prokopēn*)
	1:25	προκοπή (*prokopē*)
1:27-30	1:27	ἰδών (*idōn*), ἀκούω (*akouō*)
	1:30	εἴδετε (*eidete*), ἀκούετε (*akouete*)
2:1-18	2:2	χαράν (*charan*)
	2:18	χαίρω, συγχαίρω, χαίρετε, συγχαίρετε (*chairō, sunchairō, chairete, sunchairete*)
2:19-24	2:19	ἐν κυρίῳ (*en kuriō*), ταχέως (*tacheōs*)

31 See further D. A. Black, "The Problem of the Literary Structure of Hebrews: An Evaluation and a Proposal," *GTJ* 7 (1986) 163-77.

	2:24	ἐν κυρίῳ (*en kuriō*), ταχέως (*tacheōs*)
2:25-30	2:25	λειτουργόν (*leitourgon*)
	2:30	λειτουργίας (*leitourgias*)

In terms of Hebrews's epistolary structure, the brief personal epilogue (13:18-25) recalls numerous Pauline endings, while the doxology (13:25) is characteristically Pauline and verbally identical to Gal 1:5. The Timothy referred to in 13:23 is probably the same Timothy who had been a close associate of Paul.

To these facts we may add one final observation. It is good to bear in mind the descriptive title the author of Hebrews has given to the letter: τοῦ λόγου τῆς παρακλήσεως (*tou logou tēs paraklēseōs*, "word of exhortation," 13:22). It is noteworthy that the noun παράκλησις (*paraklēsis*) is confined to Luke (6 times), Paul (20 times), and this letter (3 times). Of special interest is Acts 13:15, where Paul and Barnabas enter the synagogue of Pisidian Antioch and are invited to give a λόγος παρακλήσεως (*logos paraklēseōs*). It was Paul and not Barnabas who delivered this "word of exhortation," which itself (Acts 13:16-41) shows numerous parallels with Hebrews. This is perhaps a clue, though a small one, that an epistle that calls itself a λόγος παρακλήσεως (*logos paraklēseōs*) is not alien to the mind of the apostle Paul. Of course, contrasts between Hebrews and the Pauline παράκλησις (*paraklēsis*) could also be cited. But arguments from formal dissimilarities must be used with the greatest caution. The author of the Gospel of John, for example, can hardly write a single page without using οὖν (*oun*) as a connecting particle, yet in 1 John the particle does not appear even once. Closer to home, the Pauline penchant for the argumentative transition τί οὖν ἐροῦμεν (*ti oun eroumen*, "What then shall we say?") in Romans (6 times in 6 chapters) is not found again in the Pauline epistles, not even in Galatians, where the mode of argumentation is so similar. Hence arguments from dissimilarity must be treated with great circumspection, since they are largely negative and are frequently based on the false assumption that an author who has written a dozen works has thereby revealed his entire theology and the full potentiality of his style.

This brief examination of the internal evidence reveals that the style and diction of Paul and the author of Hebrews are strikingly similar. Differences will very much depend on the precise relation between the author and his amanuensis.[32] The presence of certain rare stylistic devices in Hebrews (such as periodism and hyperbaton) would perhaps give a degree of plausibility to the conjecture, known to Clement and Origen, that the present stylistic form of the letter is to be traced to another hand. If such a conjecture be correct, the strongest case can be made for Luke, whose writings have at least a lexical factor in common with Hebrews. However, regardless of how far we are to think of a secretary composing the letter, what must be asserted is the demonstrable fact that the language of Hebrews and that of Paul are, "in many parts and in many ways," *sui generis*. This does not, of course, prove the Paulinity of Hebrews. It does, however, suggest that arguments fashioned to separate Hebrews from Paul on account of differences in literary style are based, not upon careful examination of the facts, but on first impressions.[33]

PART 2: THE EXTERNAL EVIDENCE

We now turn our attention to the external evidence relevant to the issue of authorship.[34] Beginning in the second century, the history of

---

32 On the role of the amanuensis in the Pauline literature, see R. N. Longe-necker, "Ancient Amanuenses and the Pauline Epistles," in *New Dimensions in New Testament Studies* (ed. R. N. Longenecker and M. C. Tenney [Grand Rapids: Zondervan, 1974] 281-97). Longenecker (294) writes: "Just how closely the apostle supervised his various amanuenses in each particular instance is, of course, impossible to say…. Paul's own practice probably varied with the specific circumstances of the case and with the particular companion whom he employed at the time."

33 F. F. Bruce (*The Epistle to the Hebrews* [NICNT; Grand Rapids: Eerdmans, 1964] xxxv-xlii) is an example of those who reject the Pauline authorship of Hebrews based not on an independent comparison of Hebrews with the Pauline writings but rather by quoting previous commentators, including Calvin. For further parallels between Paul and Hebrews, see Pitts and Walker, "The Author-ship of Hebrews," 166-71.

34 The statements of the church fathers may be found in any exegetical com-mentary on Hebrews and will therefore not be repeated here. For excellent summaries of the patristic literature, see A. B. Davidson, *The Epistle to the Hebrews* (Edinburgh: T & T Clark, n. d.) 25-34; H. A. Attridge, *The Epistle to the Hebrews* (Hermeneia; Philadelphia: Fortress) 1-6.

the canonization of Hebrews and the question of whether Paul wrote it are intermingled. Hence the question of the canonicity of the epistle is dependent somewhat on how we answer the question of authorship. However, it would be impossible to deal with both of these issues in these pages, and I shall have to limit my remarks to the statements of the fathers concerning authorship. To be sure, it has been a common practice nowadays to dismiss the evidence provided by these ancient scholars, since the church fathers can no longer be cross-examined, whereas we have access to all the internal evidence. Nevertheless, the letter is ascribed to Paul by a good number of the church fathers, who, as far as we know, had the best means of information with regard to both its genuineness and its authenticity. In investigating the external evidence, I entertain, of course, no opinion that our brief remarks will render the point in dispute certain. Rather, the question is whether there is not a probability in favor of Pauline authorship that is sufficient to quiet our reasonable doubts. This section, then, attempts to approach the question from the point of view of the external evidence, that is, from whatever can be gleaned from the ancient Christian fathers respecting the epistle's authorship.

The situation in the East requires only a brief summation, since the earliest eastern fathers insisted on affixing Paul's name to Hebrews. The first testimony that we possess comes from Pantaenus, the head of the famous catechetical school in Alexandria, as recorded by Clement, his disciple and successor, in a work entitled the *Institutions*.[35] This testimony shows (1) that Pantaenus entertained no doubts about the Pauline authorship of the letter, and (2) that he was aware of certain objections against this opinion based on the absence of the usual Pauline inscription. His answer to these objections—that Paul, being the apostle to the Gentiles, out of modesty did not want to appear to be an apostle to the Hebrews—is perhaps a poor specimen of critical reasoning, but this is no confutation of his testimony. Pantaenus does not hesitate in the least to consider it an established fact that Paul was the author of the letter, and there is no reason for him to have held to this opinion save his desire to defend the custom of the churches of his day. Thus it is that the most ancient church, in the most primitive stage of Christianity, received the letter as both Pauline and canonical—a fact to which the head of the first

---

35 This work is now lost, but we have an extract from it in Eusebius' *Ecclesiastical History*.

Christian university in the world clearly attests. That Pantaenus evoked an opinion that was general and prevalent at this period cannot be doubted.

Clement, who succeeded Pantaenus near the close of the second century, was well qualified to judge what was the general tradition of the church in respect to matters of authorship and canonicity. Suffice it to say here that Clement affirms Paul as the author of Hebrews. However, Clement also asserts that, because the letter was addressed to Hebrews, it was originally written in their language and later translated by Luke for use by the Greeks. For Clement, this fact explains both the style of the epistle and the absence of Paul's usual salutation, in that the Hebrews had conceived a prejudice against Paul. Thus Clement asserts what his predecessor Pantaenus also asserted, namely that Paul authored the epistle to the Hebrews, differing with Pantaenus only in his explanation of the letter's style by showing how the epistle can be diverse from Paul's and yet derive its origin from the apostle. This solution, it seems to me, is a much more probable one than that of Pantaenus; but the main point to be observed here is that the objection raised from style was felt to be far from adverse to genuine Pauline authorship.

Thus at the close of the second century the epistle to the Hebrews not only existed as a canonical writing, but a firm belief existed that Paul was its author, a belief that harmonized with the general opinion of the church, which required evidence of apostolic origin or at least apostolic approbation in order to include a certain writing in its canon.

We may now advance to Origen, the disciple and successor of Clement at Alexandria, whose testimony has also been preserved by Eusebius. The sentiments of Origen in regard to the authorship of Hebrews may be summarized as follows:

» Origen meets the stylistic objection to Pauline authorship in a manner similar to that of Clement: the thoughts are to be regarded as Pauline, but the style and diction are to be credited to another hand. In this way Origen maintains the apostolic origin of the epistle while apparently removing the objection drawn from the diversity of style.

» When Origen says, "It is not without reason that the ancients handed it down as Paul's," and then adds, "but who wrote the epistle, in truth God knows, some attributing it to Luke, and some to Clement," it could not be more obvious that he means to suggest uncertainty only concerning the penman (or "stenographer," a term preferred by Pitts and Walker)—that is, the one who reduced the letter to writing—for he has just asserted that the thoughts are those of the apostle Paul. To assert (as is often asserted) that Origen meant to suggest that only God knew the *author* of the epistle is to suppose that Origen has contradicted himself in the selfsame paragraph.

» It is beyond question that Origen bases his own belief regarding the Pauline authorship of our epistle, and the belief of the churches of his time, on the most ancient tradition. Though he, like others before him, struggled between his own conviction of Pauline authorship and the diversity of style between Hebrews and the Pauline writings, he consistently quoted the letter as being Paul's and indeed commended those churches that held to Pauline authorship on the basis of the truly ancient tradition (see Appendix: Origen on the Authorship of Hebrews). However, for Origen the identity of the amanuensis or translator of Paul was a subordinate matter. The νοήματα (*noēmata*) belonged to Paul; the φράσις (*phrasis*) and σύνθεσις (*sunthesis*) belonged to someone else. But it is the matter of the νοήματα (*noēmata*) that is vital and that settles all the questions that can be of any great consequence.

The subsequent opinion of the Alexandrian and Egyptian churches appears to have been the same regarding the authorship of our epistle, and no serious doubts existed after the time of Origen in regard to its Pauline origin. The belief that Paul was the author of Hebrews was universal also in the non-Egyptian eastern churches, Eusebius of Caesarea himself claiming Paul as the author ("Fourteen epistles are clearly and certainly Paul's")—a claim that is unequivocal: πρόδηλοι καὶ σαφεῖς (*prodēloi kai sapheis*). Those who dissent from this opinion, writes Eusebius, base their views not on the testimony of the oriental fathers, but on the alleged example of the church in Rome.

Other testimonies might be named, but they would be superfluous. The unity and universality of the opinion in the church in all the East that Paul wrote the epistle will certainly be admitted by every unprejudiced mind. Individuals indeed existed who denied the letter's authenticity, but no respectable or widely diffused opinion ever existed.

In the West a different state of affairs existed, at least in the earliest centuries. That the letter was known in the western churches in the late first and early second centuries is clear from the evidence provided by

Clement of Rome and the Old Latin Version. It was not until the latter part of the second century that a hint of negative evidence is to be found, and this is in the testimony of Irenaeus, the bishop of Lyons and former disciple of Polycarp. That Irenaeus quoted the book of Hebrews cannot be doubted, but whether he regarded the letter as canonical is uncertain. It is, however, from the works of Tertullian that clear doubts about the apostolic origin of Hebrews can be adduced. He ascribed the letter to Barnabas and therefore refused to grant it full canonical status, the epistle (he felt) not being the work of an apostle. It is also probable that churches in other areas of North Africa doubted or denied the Pauline authorship of Hebrews. Later on, however, the epistle was admitted to be Paul's by the Councils of Hippo (AD 393) and Carthage (AD 397), as well as in the lists of canonical books set forth in their canons. These canons speak of thirteen epistles of Paul, and then add, "[he wrote] another one to the Hebrews." In addition, Hebrews was clearly received as Paul's by Hilary (AD 354), Lucifer (AD 354), Victorinus (AD 360), Ambrose (AD 374), Philaster (AD 380), Gaudentius (AD 387), and Rufinus (AD 397).

It was the testimony of Jerome and Augustine that seems to have been most influential in establishing the apostolicity of Hebrews among the western churches. Both of these ancient scholars knew that some of the Latin churches doubted the letter's authenticity or at least its Pauline origin, yet the authority of the eastern churches moved them to receive the epistle as canonical. The tradition in the West that there were thirteen epistles of Paul clearly meant *thirteen that bear the apostle's name*. The fifth Council of Carthage (AD 419), in fact, reckoned *fourteen* epistles as Paul's, without any further qualification.

Let us now attempt to summarize our findings based on the external evidence. In spite of doubts in some western minds, the earliest church insisted on affixing Paul's name to Hebrews. They did not, however, exclude the possibility that another mind may have contributed to give the letter its peculiar beauty of form. Clement, the head of the catechetical school in Alexandria, received Hebrews from his predecessor Pantaenus as an epistle of Paul, though Clement also adopted the theory of a Hebrew original that was later translated into Greek by Luke.

That Clement's suggestions did not have the force of a tradition is seen in the fact that his pupil Origen abandoned it and adopted another theory, namely that the thoughts of the letter were Paul's, but its style and composition belonged to someone else. Origen was aware of two conjectures, one identifying the assistant as Clement of Rome, the other identifying him as Luke. Nevertheless, on the strength of the ecclesiastical tradition that he had inherited from the "ancients" (ἀρχαῖοι ἄνδρες, *archaioi andres*), Origen constantly cited the epistle as Paul's. But as to the identity of the penman, that is, the one who wrote (ὁ γράψας, *ho grapsas*) the epistle, "Τὸ μὲν ἀληθὲς θεὸς οἶδεν" (*"to men alēthes theos oiden"*).[36]

With the words ὁ γράψας (*ho grapsas*) Origen could hardly have meant full authorship, for he plainly attributes a certain authorship to Paul and, as we have said, consistently cites the letter as Paul's. The words ὁ γράψας (*ho grapsas*) must therefore denote the writer to whom the letter owes its present form. This is not widely different from the sense in which ὁ γράψας (*ho grapsas*) is used in Rom 16:22 in connection with Tertius, the writer (though not the author) of Romans.

As for the witness of the western fathers, this testimony is chiefly negative, yet even here there is doubt and uncertainty rather than outright opposition, even though Tertullian felt the epistle to have been written by Barnabas. This uncertainty prevailed in the West until the middle of the fourth century, at which time the tide of opinion began to change. Soon afterwards the epistle was acknowledged to be Pauline by Hilary of Poitiers and by several other western writers of note. After the time of Jerome (c. 392), the apostolic origin of Hebrews was generally acknowledged in the western church. Thus Augustine, influenced by the authority of the eastern churches (*auctoritas ecclesiarum orientalum*), could reckon the letter to the Hebrews among the fourteen epistles of Paul, because the arguments against its canonicity did not appear to him to be convincing.

From these observations the following conclusions seem evident:

1. In the East, where the epistle was apparently first received and where its historical circumstances were best understood, Hebrews was from the beginning endorsed by most ecclesiastical writers as an epistle of Paul, thus passing into the NT canon of the eastern churches without question.

---

36 See Eusebius, *Ecclesiastical History*, 6.25.14: τίς δὲ ὁ γράψας τὴν ἐπιστολήν, τὸ μὲν ἀληθὲς θεὸς οἶδεν (*tis de ho grapsas tēn epistolēn, to men alēthes theos oiden*), "But who wrote the epistle, in truth God knows."

2. For a time many of the western fathers were doubtful concerning it, but after more mature investigation the churches in the West, along with those of the East, were constrained to admit its Pauline authorship. Possibly the use made of Hebrews by the Montanists, who welcomed its denial of a second repentance, compromised the letter in certain quarters.[37] Especially the passages in Heb 6:4-8 and 10:26-31 seem strongly to favor the views that they maintained. The church at Rome carried the dispute against the Montanists to a very high degree. It must therefore be allowed as not improbable that the epistle to the Hebrews may in this way have become obnoxious to the Roman church. If one desires similar instances of this in the history of the church, one need only point to the rejection of the Apocalypse by many eastern writers on account of their opposition to the Chiliasts who made so much use of it, or to Luther's rejection of the epistle of James because he viewed it as thwarting his notion of justification, even going so far as to give it the appellation of *epistola straminea* ("epistle of straw").

3. Even though Origen experienced doubts about the penman of Hebrews, he seems to agree with the "ancients" that the thoughts are Paul's, and that he is therefore the real and proper author of the epistle. Let it not be forgotten that the church to whom our epistle was addressed must have known the identity of the author, as chapter

---

37 So J. Moffatt, A *Critical and Exegetical Commentary on the Epistle to the Hebrews* (ICC; Edinburgh: T & T Clark, 1924) xx. Cf. W. L. Lane, *Hebrews 1-8* (WBC 47A; Dallas: Word, 1991) clii-cliii: "It may well be that the rigor with which the writer argued for the impossibility of repentance after apostasy accounts for its relative neglect in the second and third centuries in the West, and the reluctance of the Western Church to acknowledge its authority under pressure from the East in the fourth century." A slightly different account of the external evidence is given by F. Delitzch, *Commentary on the Epistle to the Hebrews* (Edinburgh: T & T Clark, 1868) 11: "The abuse made by Arians and Novatians of several passages had prejudiced the West against the epistle, and that still more from the circumstance that no ancient Western tradition spoke in its favor. But these prejudices gradually gave way as a better exegesis showed the goundlessness of the heretical misinterpretations, and as the ever-increasing intercourse between the churches of East and West, which the Arian controversies induced, made the consensus of the Oriental churches in favour [sic] of the apostolic authorship better known to their Western brethren."

13 makes plain. Would not the fame of this have reached Alexandria, the second metropolis of the world? And would not the memory of it have been perpetuated in the famous school there, down to future generations? We do not insist this is so; but we can provide no other explanation of the fact that the churches in Alexandria were uniform in their belief that Paul was the author.

This conclusion based on the external evidence is, we believe, corroborated by the internal evidence. While we are willing to admit that the style of Hebrews is in some ways unlike that of Paul, we are also constrained to think that the force of this argument from dissimilarity has been greatly overrated, especially if we give to Luke, as Paul's amanuensis, a degree of liberty with regard to the letter's phraseology. The absence of Paul's name in the opening salutation finds a convincing explanation in the writings of Clement of Alexandria, who accounted for the absence of the Pauline superscription by saying that "in writing for Hebrews who had conceived a prejudice against him and suspected him, he very prudently did not put them off at the outset by setting down his name."[38]

If Clement's assessment is correct, then Paul, setting about to prove that Judaism had come to an end through the fulfillment of the law by Christ, did so without using his apostolic revelations but solely on the basis of what anyone in his audience could read from the OT. In this way he underplayed the direct revelation of the gospel that came to the apostles (2:3), for he could not allude to his closer knowledge of the gospel without revealing his authority and hence his identity, thus prejudicing the readers against his epistle immediately.

CONCLUSION

Looking back over the ground covered by this somewhat tedious exposition, one cannot but be struck by the enormous amount of thought that is common to Hebrews and Paul. The use of Hab 2:4 (used only in Romans, Galatians, and Hebrews) alone is enough to give one pause before rejecting Pauline authorship. A further examination would reveal that there is no teaching in Hebrews that is incompatible with that of the apostle Paul. Differences of emphasis may indeed be detected, but the

---

38 Eusebius, *Ecclesiastical History*, 6.14.3.

absence of some particular Pauline idea is itself merely a negative thing and can furnish no positive argument against Pauline authorship.[39]

In view of the numerous affinities between Hebrews and Paul, it seems to us a most unlikely hypothesis that any other mind than the apostle's could have propounded truth on such harmoniously Pauline lines. Of the other leading candidates for authorship—Barnabas, Luke, and Apollos—none seems to have possessed the thorough knowledge of Judaism required for writing this letter. Tertullian's conjecture that Barnabas was the author had no basis in tradition. The western church, had it really believed the epistle to be the composition of Barnabas, would not so easily have set it aside. Moreover, Barnabas does not appear in the NT as capable of writing such a treatise as Hebrews. Under pressure from the Judaizers he had wavered theologically at Antioch (Gal 2:13), and he is portrayed in Acts as a loving encourager but not as a spokesman or teacher (Acts 14:12). Luke too seems to lack the intimate knowledge of Judaism that the author of Hebrews possessed. The main difficulty with Luke, however, is the lack of any external evidence that he was the author, for Origen's statement that either Luke or Clement "wrote" the epistle seems to preclude Luke from being the immediate author of Hebrews inasmuch as Origen consistently cites the letter as Paul's. Thus the theory that Luke was an independent author has no right to appeal to antiquity and must stand entirely on the very inadequate grounds of internal probabilities afforded by language and style. Finally, for Luther's conjecture that Apollos wrote Hebrews—a view that has secured the adherence of many distinguished writers on the epistle—there is no ecclesiastical tradition and no possible way of testing its truth. Perhaps the strongest argument against Apollos is the fact that the church in Alexandria never credited him with authorship, even though he was an Alexandrian Jew and a man "mighty in the Scriptures" (Acts 18:24).

We may contrast all of this with the case for Paul. Although Paul saw himself as the Apostle to the Gentiles, he preached to the Jews first wherever he went (Rom 1:16), often visited the Jerusalem church, and had a deep spiritual concern for Israel (Rom 9:1-5; 10:1-4). His Pharisaical training in Jerusalem under Gamaliel would have provided him

---

39 Thus, for example, the concept of the church as Christ's body, so prevalent in Ephesians and Colossians, is as much absent from Philippians, their immediate contemporary, as it is from Hebrews.

with a thorough knowledge of the Jewish sacrificial system, and few others would have had the background to compose such a book heavy with allusions to Exodus and Leviticus. Therefore, since the internal evidence is not unfavorable to Pauline authorship, and since the external evidence is largely in its support, the best course of action in our view is to accept that Hebrews was authored by Paul the apostle, possibly with the assistance of an amanuensis such as Luke.

In conclusion, we have examined the main reasons from the epistle itself that seem to favor Pauline authorship. That they are not conclusive we readily agree. But still they carry considerable weight and serve to corroborate the conclusion drawn from the external evidence that Hebrews is in all probability one of Paul's own epistles. Indeed, the concurrence of both kinds of evidence is such as to afford grounds of probability as strong as could be expected in regard to a question so ancient and so difficult. Direct and positive proof, incapable of being in any way questioned or contradicted, can neither be required nor justly expected. But there is sufficient evidence to render the opinion of the ancient church altogether probable. That Luke may have been Paul's amanuensis and with Paul's consent have modified the style of the apostle is not improbable. But unless we ignore the testimony of the earliest Christian fathers we are constrained to conclude that Paul himself is the real author of this epistle.

If the question, then, is asked whether in spite of the perpetual, unanimous, and constant assertion of the eastern fathers, with which the entire western church entered into complete agreement after the 4th century, such force is to be attributed to the doubts discussed above as to justify hesitation in receiving this letter not only among the canonical writings but also as a letter to be placed among the genuine writings of the apostle Paul, the present writer would answer with an emphatic No. History says that Paul is the author of Hebrews; but as for the secondary hand, his identity will have to be left in the future, as in the past, to divine omniscience.[40]

---

40 A slightly different conclusion arises for the authorship of the Gospel according to Mark. The apostle Peter is the author, while Mark served as his stenographer. This is clear from the patristic testimony. See my *Why Four Gospels? The Historical Origins of the Gospels* (Gonzalez, FL: Energion, 2010).

APPENDIX: ORIGEN ON THE AUTHORSHIP OF HEBREWS

We have seen that Origen meets the stylistic objection to Pauline authorship in a manner similar to that of his predecessor Clement: the *thoughts* are Pauline, but the *style and diction* are to be credited to another hand. When he says, "For not without reason have the men of old handed it down as Paul's," and then adds, "But who wrote the epistle, in truth God knows," he does not mean to imply uncertainty about the *author* but only about the *penman*—that is, the one who reduced the letter to writing—for he has just asserted that the thoughts are those of the apostle Paul. To maintain that Origen meant to suggest that only God knew the *author* of the epistle is to suppose that Origen has contradicted himself in the very same paragraph.

It is astonishing to see how these basic facts about Origen's view of authorship are overlooked by commentators on Hebrews, who almost always quote him in support of an agnostic position on the letter's authorship (and, by extension, its conceptual background). It is clear that Origen is referring, not to the author responsible for the contents of the letter, but to its penman, and he is certain that the former is none other than the apostle Paul. Had these authors read the works of Origen they would have seen that his actual method of quoting Hebrews indicates a firm belief in the Pauline authorship of the letter. A sampling of quotations from Origen will make this clear.

De Principiis 1:

And therefore I think it sufficient to quote this one testimony of **Paul** from the Epistle to the Hebrews, in which he says [Heb 11:24-26], "By faith Moses, when he was come to years, refused to be called the son of Pharaoh's daughter; choosing rather to suffer affliction with the people of God, than to enjoy the pleasures of sin for a season; esteeming the reproach of Christ greater riches than the treasures of the Egyptians."

33

De Principiis 3.2.4:

And **the apostle Paul** warns us [Heb 2:1]: "Therefore we ought to give the more earnest heed to the things which we have heard, lest perhaps we should let them slip."

De Principiis 4.1.13:

In another Epistle also, when referring to the tabernacle, **he [Paul]** mentions the direction which was given to Moses [Heb 8:5]: "Thou shalt make (all things) according to the pattern which was showed thee in the mount."

De Principiis 4.1.13:

Moreover, in the Epistle to the Hebrews, discoursing of those who belong to the circumcision, **he [Paul]** writes [Heb 8:5]: "who serve for an ensample and shadow of heavenly things."

De Principiis 4.1.24:

For **Paul** openly says of them [Heb 8:5], that "they serve unto the example and shadow of heavenly things."

De Principiis 2.6.7:

And **the apostle [Paul]** says with reference to the law [Heb 8:5], that they who have circumcision of the flesh, "serve for the similitude and shadow of heavenly things."

De Principiis 2.3.5:

I will show, however, from what **statements of Paul** I have arrived at this understanding. He says [Heb 9:26], "But now once in the consummation of ages, He was manifested to take away sin by the sacrifice of Himself."

34

De Principiis 3.1.10:

To show more clearly, however, what we mean, let us take the illustration employed by **the apostle Paul** in the Epistle to the Hebrews, where he says [Heb 6:7-8], "For the earth, which drinketh in the rain that cometh oft upon it, and bringeth forth herbs meet for them by whom it is dressed, will receive blessing from God; but that which beareth thorns and briers is rejected, and is nigh unto cursing, whose end is to be burned."

Against Celsus 7.29:

And it is in reference to this Jerusalem that **the apostle [Paul]** spoke, as one who, "being risen with Christ, and seeking those things which are above," had found a truth which formed no part of the Jewish mythology. "Ye are come," says he [Heb 12:22], "unto Mount Sion, and unto the city of the living God, the heavenly Jerusalem, and to an innumerable company of angels."

Against Celsus 3.53:

For the word is used **by our Paul** in writing to the Corinthians, who were Greeks, and not yet purified in their morals.... Now the same writer, knowing that there was a certain kind of nourishment better adapted for the soul, and that the food of those young persons who were admitted was compared to milk, continues [Heb 5:12-14]: "And ye are become such as have need of milk, and not of strong meat. For every one that useth milk is unskilful in the word of righteousness; for he is a babe. But strong meat belongeth to them that are of full age, even those who by reason of use have their senses exercised to discern both good and evil."

To Africanus 9:

For **the author of the Epistle** to the Hebrews, in speaking of the prophets, and what they suffered, says [Heb 11:37], "they were stoned, they were sawn asunder, they were slain with the sword." [S]ome one hard pressed by this argument may have recourse to the opinion of those who reject this Epistle as not being Paul's; against whom I must at some other time use other arguments to prove that **it is Paul's.**"

Commentary on Matthew 11.12:

For **the apostle [Paul]**, however, knowing that it is not the nature of meats which is the cause of injury to him who uses them or of advantage to him who refrains from their use, but opinions and the reason which is in them, said [1 Cor. 8:8], "But meat commendeth us not to God, for neither if we eat are we the better, nor if we eat not are we the worse." And since he knew that those who have a loftier conception of what things are pure and what impure according to the law, turning aside from the distinction about the use of things pure and impure, and superstition, I think, in respect of things being different, become indifferent to the use of meats, and on this account are condemned by the Jews as transgressors of law, he said therefore, somewhere [Col. 2:16], "Let no man therefore judge you in meat or in drink," etc., teaching us that the things according to the letter are a shadow, but that the true thoughts of the law which are stored up in them are the good things to come, in which one may find what are the pure spiritual meats of the soul, and what are the impure foods in false and contradictory words which injure the man who is nourished in them [Heb. 10:1], "For the law had a shadow of the good things to come."

Commentary on John 1.3:

Here some one may object that it is somewhat too bold to apply the name of high-priests to men, when Jesus Himself is spoken of in many a prophetic passage as the one great priest, as [Heb. 4:14], "We have a great high-priest who has passed through the heavens, Jesus, the Son of God." But to this we reply that **the apostle [Paul]** clearly defined this meaning, and declared the prophet to have said about the Christ [Heb. 5:6], "Thou art a priest for ever, according to the order of Melchisedek," and not according to the order of Aaron.

Commentary on John 1.20:

There is also an arche in a matter of learning, as when we say that the letters are the arche of grammar. **The apostle [Paul]** accordingly says [Heb. 5:12]: "When by reason of the time you ought to be teachers, you have need again that some one teach you what are the elements of the arche of the oracles of God."

Commentary on John 1.23:

According to **Paul**, too, He is declared to be the wisdom and the power of God, as in the Epistle to the Corinthians: "Christ the power of God and the wisdom of God." It is added that He is also sanctification and redemption: "He was made to us of God," he says, "wisdom and righteousness and sanctification and redemption." But **he [Paul]** also teaches us, writing to the Hebrews, that Christ is a High-Priest [Heb. 4:14]: "Having, therefore, a great High-Priest, who has passed through the heavens, Jesus the Son of God, let us hold fast our profession."

Commentary on John 2.11:

For it was a great gift to the Patriarchs that God in place of His own name should add their name to His own designation as God, as **Paul** says [Heb. 11:16], "Therefore God is not ashamed to be called their God."

Commentary on John 6.32:

Now that the principle of the sacrifice must be apprehended with reference to certain heavenly mysteries, appears from the words of **the apostle [Paul]**, who somewhere says [Heb. 8:5], "Who serve a pattern and shadow of heavenly things,"

37

and again [Heb 9:23], "It was necessary that the patterns of the things in the heavens should be purified with these, but the heavenly things themselves with better sacrifices than these."

These examples are sufficient to show that Origen, in his extant works, ascribes the authorship of Hebrews to the apostle Paul. He knew that the ancients had handed Hebrews down as a Pauline epistle, and it was on the strength of that tradition that he constantly cited the letter as Paul's and declared his readiness to prove his convictions by arguments. Origen was aware of two conjectures, one identifying the assistant as Clement of Rome, the other identifying him as Luke. Nevertheless, on the strength of the ecclesiastical tradition that he had inherited from the "men of old," Origen consistently cited the epistle as Paul's. In light of this fact, any further attempt to use Origen's words in support of an agnostic position on the authorship of Hebrews is not to quote Origen, but to misquote him.

www.ingramcontent.com/pod-product-compliance
Lightning Source LLC
Chambersburg PA
CBHW011749020426
42331CB00014B/3334